Alfred's Basic Piano Library

Christmas Book · Le[v]

MW01012168

P ✦ i a n o

Selected and Edited by E. L. Lancaster & Morton Manus

This book may be used by students in Level 2 of Alfred's Basic Piano Library or in the third book of any method.

The enduring charm of the Christmas season brings out the need for composers to express their feelings in newly-created Christmas music each year. Many of these 20th-century songs are as well-known and loved as the traditional carols.

For this *Top Hits Christmas* series (Levels 1A, 1B, 2, 3, 4) we have selected only those new musical favorites that have become a permanent part of the Christmas season, and arranged them for young piano students. When combined with the traditional carols available in Alfred's *Merry Christmas!* Series (Levels 1A, 1B, 2, 3, 4), piano students have at their fingertips all the music they would want to perform during the holiday season.

PROGRESSIVE ORDER: When Christmas music can teach and reinforce the musical concepts students are studying, it is doubly beneficial. There is no need to play pieces above or below the appropriate grade level, or to take a break from proper piano study, to enjoy playing Christmas music.

With this in mind, this book has been written to fit with the music fundamentals as they are introduced in Level 2 of Alfred's Basic Piano Library. Since the melodies and rhythms of popular music do not always lend themselves to precise grading, you may find that these pieces are sometimes a little more difficult than the corresponding pages in the Lesson Book. Although the songs are placed in approximate order of difficulty, they may be played in any order. The teacher's judgment is the most important factor in deciding when to begin each title.

The arrangers and editors wish the teacher, student and parents a very merry Christmas and hope you will enjoy the new and special arrangements of Christmas music found in this book.

Published by

HAL·LEONARD®
CORPORATION

Distributed by
Alfred Music

ISBN 0-7390-0401-8

The Chipmunk Song

Words and Music by Ross Bagdasarian
Arr. by Tom Gerou

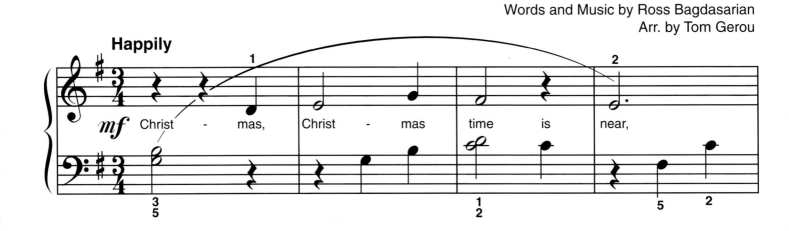

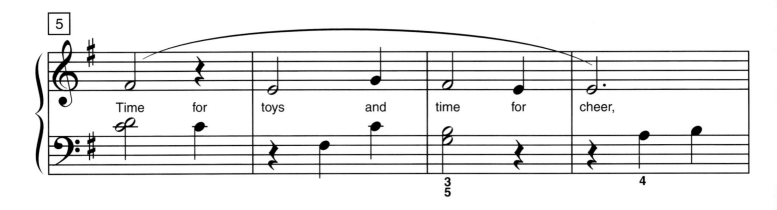

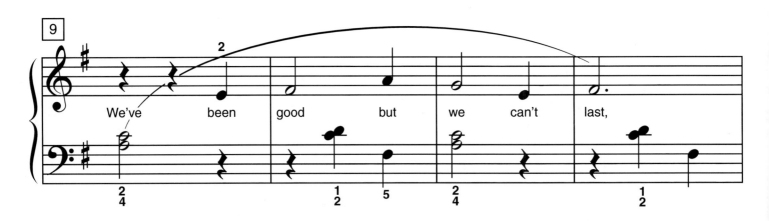

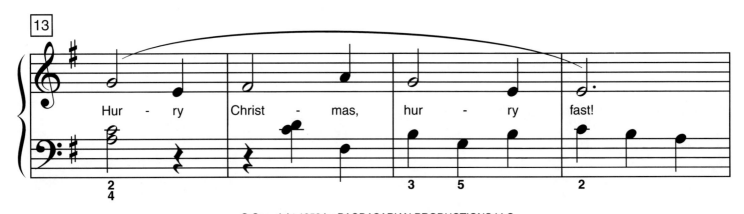

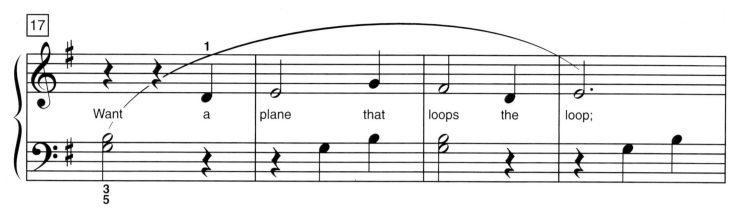

17
Want a plane that loops the loop;

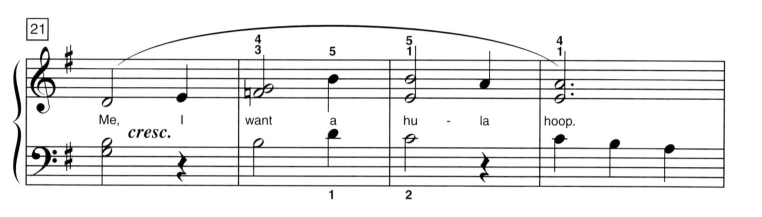

21
Me, *cresc.* I want a hu - la hoop.

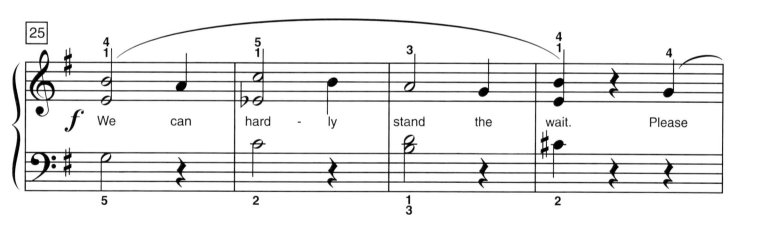

25
f We can hard - ly stand the wait. Please

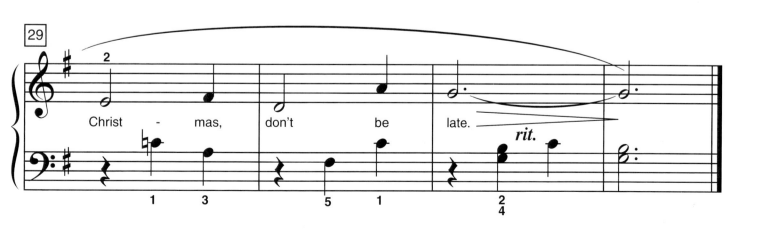

29
Christ - mas, don't be late. *rit.*

When Santa Claus Gets Your Letter

Music and Lyrics by Johnny Marks
Arr. by Sharon Aaronson

Moderato

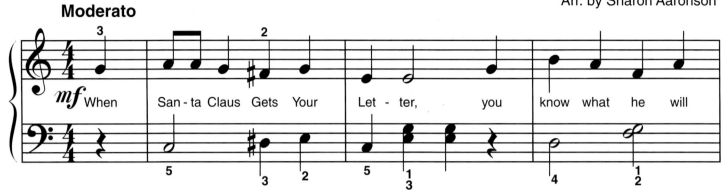

When San-ta Claus Gets Your Let - ter, you know what he will

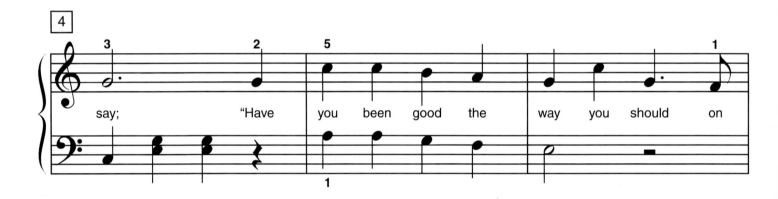

say; "Have you been good the way you should on

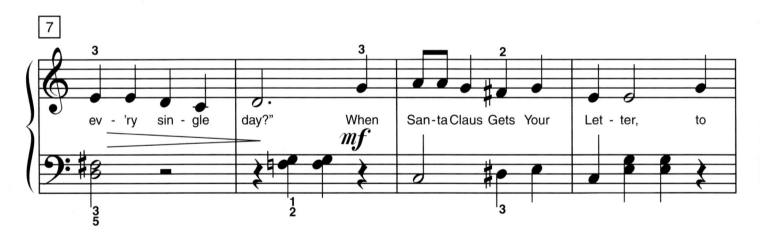

ev - 'ry sin - gle day?" When San-ta Claus Gets Your Let - ter, to

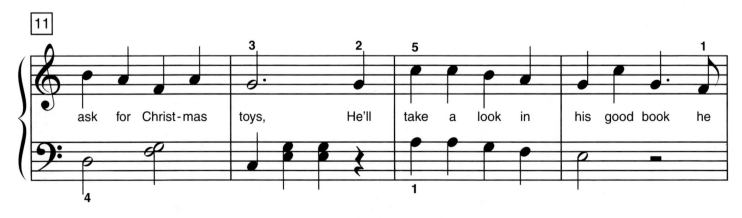

ask for Christ-mas toys, He'll take a look in his good book he

Frosty the Snow Man

Words and Music by
Steve Nelson and Jack Rollins
Arr. by Tom Gerou

Rudolph the Red-Nosed Reindeer

Music and Lyrics by Johnny Marks
Arr. by Dennis Alexander

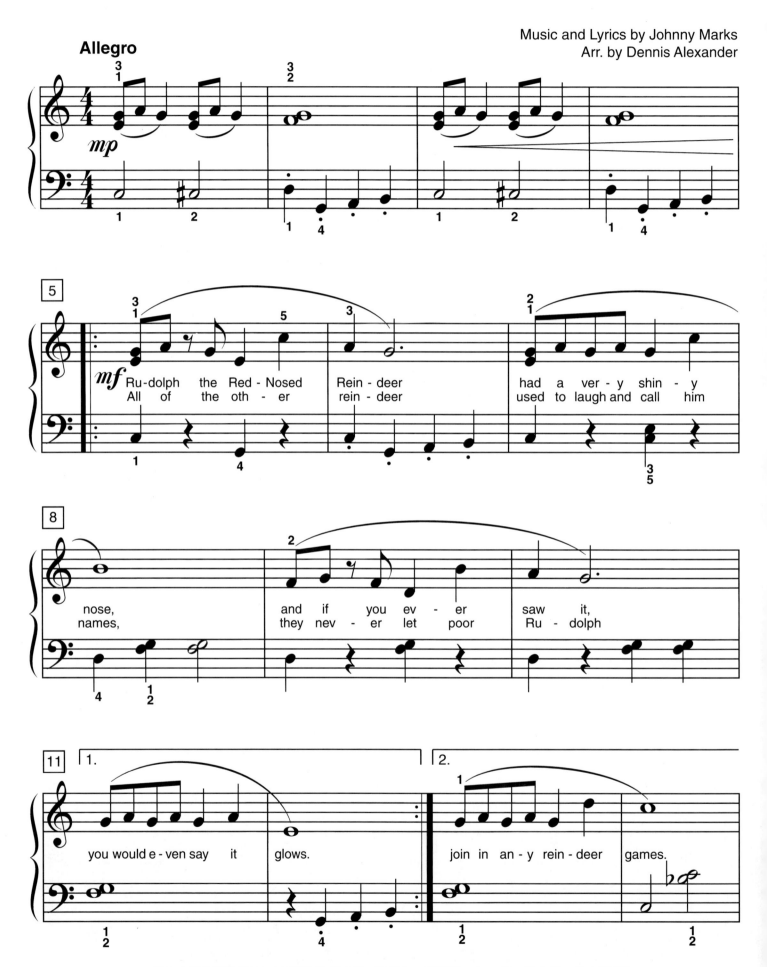

Ru-dolph the Red - Nosed Rein - deer had a ver - y shin - y
All of the oth - er rein - deer used to laugh and call him

nose, and if you ev - er saw it,
names, they nev - er let poor Ru - dolph

1. you would e - ven say it glows.

2. join in an - y rein - deer games.

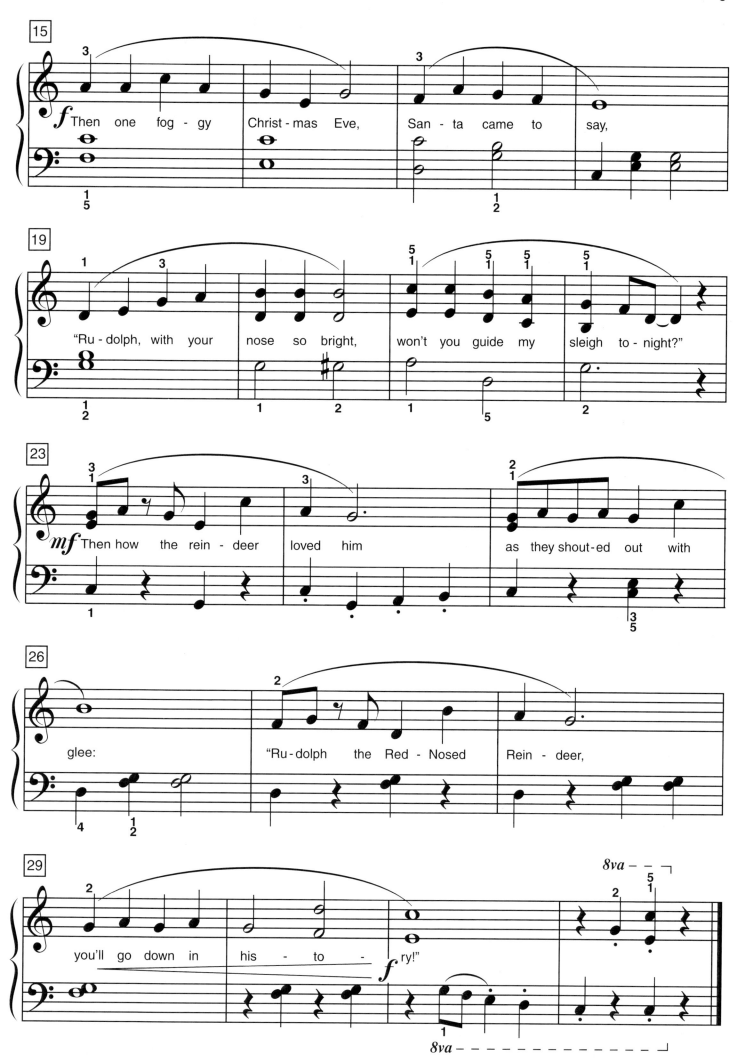

Rockin' Around the Christmas Tree

Music and Lyrics by Johnny Marks
Arr. by George Peter Tingley

*Optional: Play eighth notes a bit unevenly,
in a "lilting" style: long short long short, *etc.*

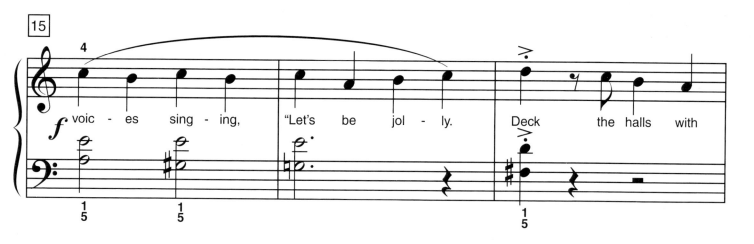

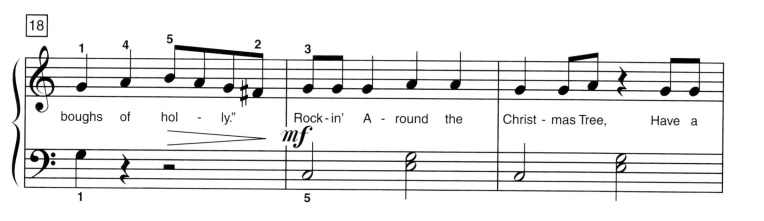

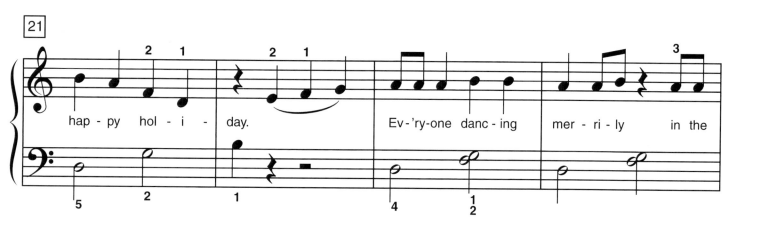

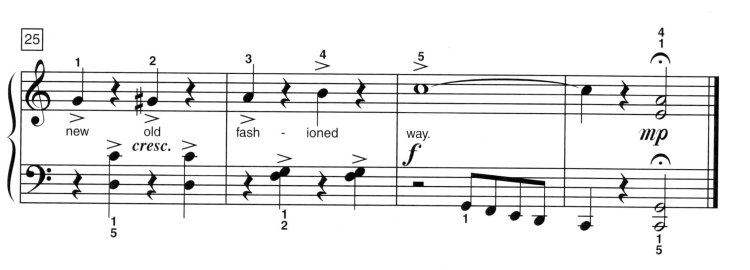

Mister Santa

Words and Music by Pat Ballard
Arr. by George Peter Tingley

Bright and brisk

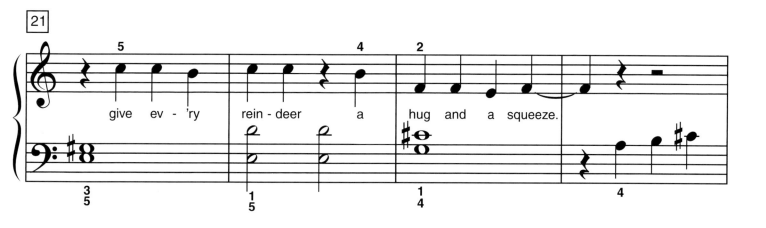

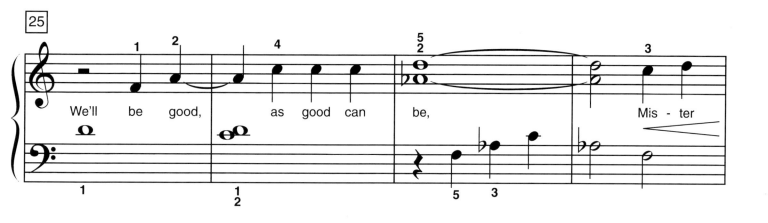

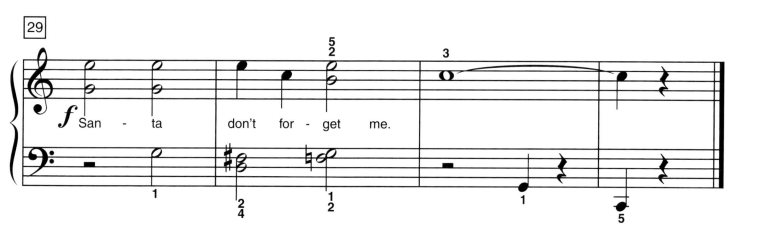

Nuttin' for Christmas

Words and Music by
Roy Bennett and Sid Tepper
Arr. by Tom Gerou

2. I put a tack on teacher's chair; somebody snitched on me.
   I tied a knot in Susie's hair; somebody snitched on me.
   I did a dance on Mommy's plants, climbed a tree and tore my pants.
   Filled the sugar bowl with ants; somebody snitched on me. So, ...

3. I won't be seeing Santa Claus; somebody snitched on me.
   He won't come visit me because somebody snitched on me.
   Next year I'll be going straight, next year I'll be good, just wait.
   I'd start now but it's too late; somebody snitched on me. Oh, ...

Let It Snow! Let It Snow! Let It Snow!

Words by Sammy Cahn
Music by Jule Styne
Arr. by Martha Mier

*Optional: Play eighth notes a bit unevenly,
in a "lilting" style: long short long short, *etc.*

(There's No Place Like)
Home for the Holidays

Words by Al Stillman
Music by Robert Allen
Arr. by Sharon Aaronson

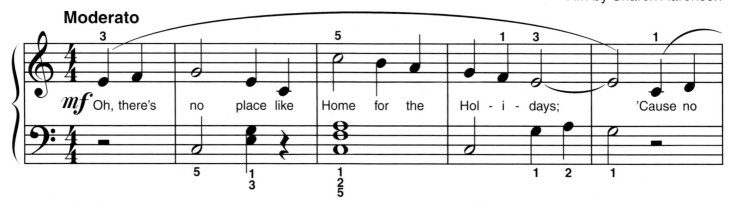

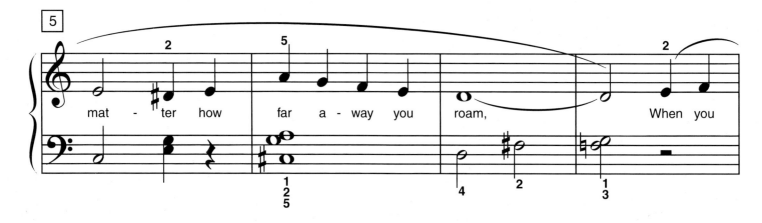

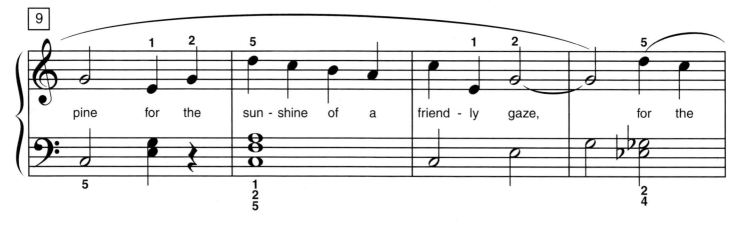

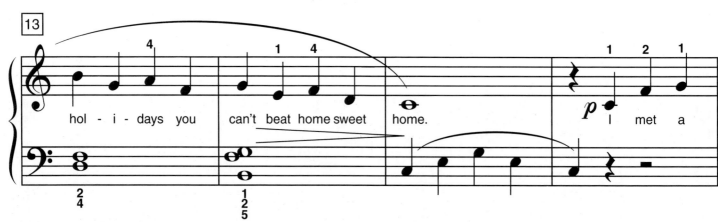

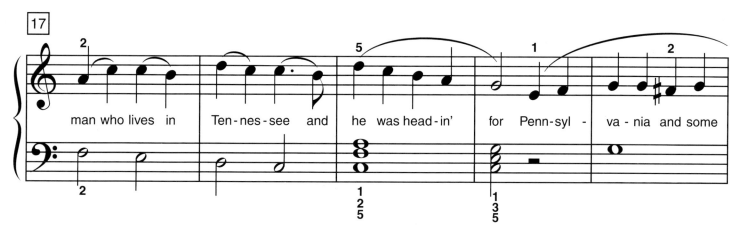

man who lives in Ten-nes-see and he was head-in' for Penn-syl - va - nia and some

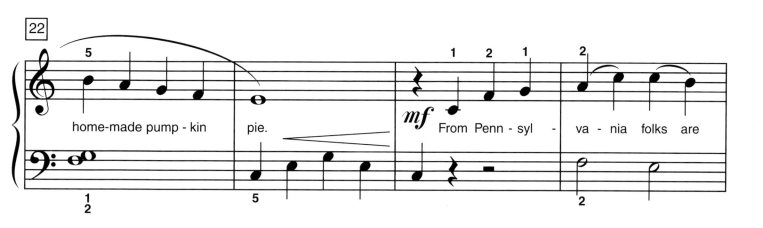

home-made pump-kin pie. *mf* From Penn-syl - va - nia folks are

trav - 'lin' down to Dix - ie's sun - ny shores; From At - lan - tic to Pa -

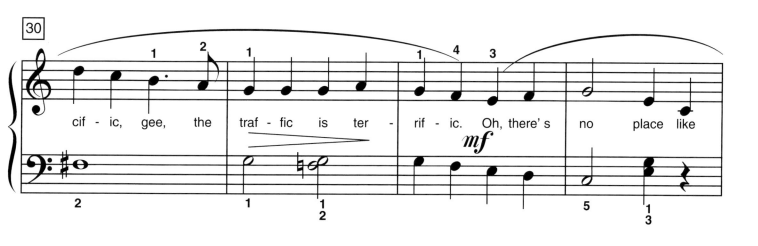

cif - ic, gee, the traf - fic is ter - rif - ic. Oh, there's no place like

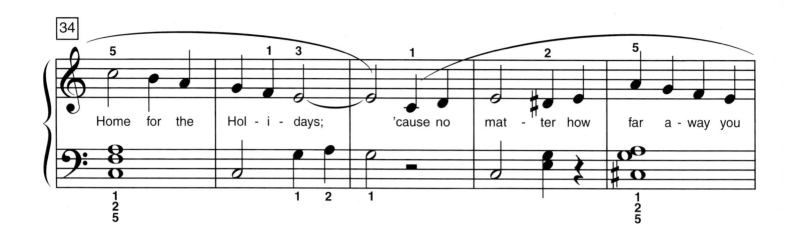

Home for the Hol - i - days; 'cause no mat - ter how far a - way you

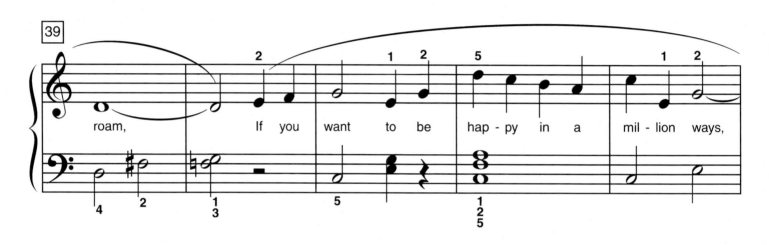

roam, If you want to be hap - py in a mil - lion ways,

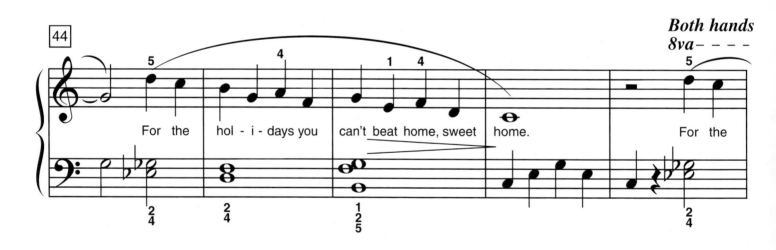

Both hands
8va - - - -

For the hol - i - days you can't beat home, sweet home. For the

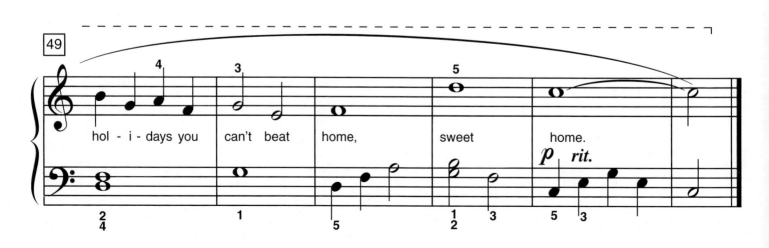

hol - i - days you can't beat home, sweet home.

p *rit.*

Feliz Navidad

Music and Lyrics by Jose Feliciano
Arr. by George Peter Tingley

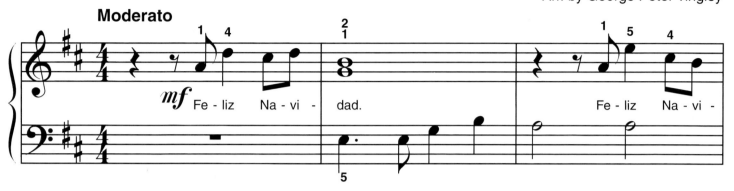

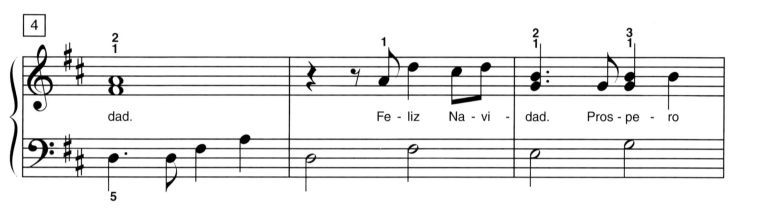

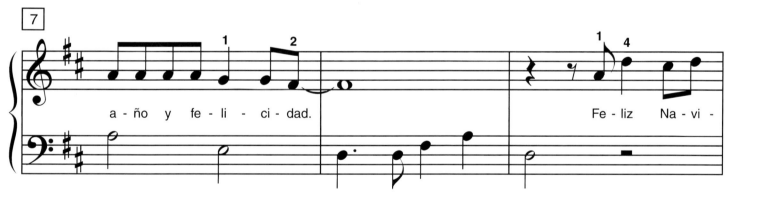

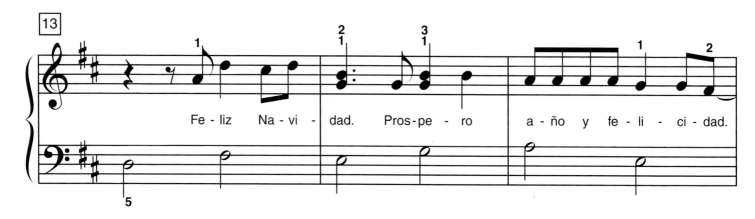

Fe - liz Na - vi - dad. Pros-pe - ro a - ño y fe - li - ci - dad.

I want to wish you a Mer - ry Christ - mas,

with lots of pres - ents to make you hap - py. I want to wish you a

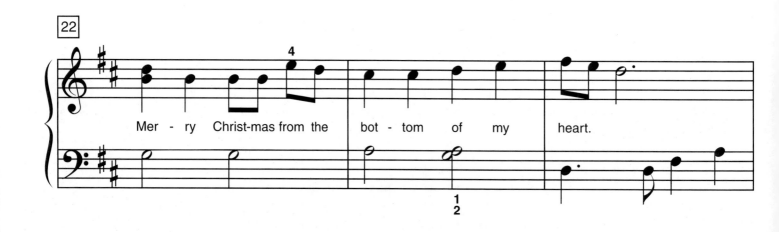

Mer - ry Christ-mas from the bot - tom of my heart.